HARUNOBU

MASTERWORKS OF UKIYO-E

春信

HARUNOBU

by Seiichirō Takahashi

English adaptation by John Bester

KODANSHA INTERNATIONAL LTD.

Tokyo, New York & San Francisco

Distributors:

UNITED STATES: Harper & Row, Publishers, Inc., 10 East 53rd Street, New York, New York 10022. SOUTH AMERICA: Harper & Row, International Department. CANADA: Fitzhenry & Whiteside Limited, 150 Lesmill Road, Don Mills, Ontario. MEXICO & CENTRAL AMERICA: HARLA S. A. de C. V., Apartado 30–546, Mexico 4, D. F. BRITISH COMMONWEALTH (excluding Canada & the Far East): TABS, 7 Maiden Lane, London WC2. EUROPE: Boxerbooks Inc., Limmatstrasse 111, 8031 Zurich. AUSTRALIA & NEW ZEALAND: Book Wise (Australia) Pty. Ltd., 104–8 Sussex Street, Sydney. THAILAND: Central Department Store Ltd., 306 Silom Road, Bangkok. HONG KONG & SINGAPORE: Books for Asia Ltd., 30 Tat Chee Avenue, Kowloon; 65 Cresscent Road, Singapore 15. THE FAR EAST: Japan Publications Trading Company, P.O. Box 5030, Tokyo International, Tokyo.

Published by Kodansha International Ltd., 2–12–21 Otowa, Bunkyo-ku, Tokyo 112 and Kodansha International/USA, Ltd., 10 East 53rd Street, New York, New York 10022 and 44 Montgomery Street, San Francisco, California 94104. Copyright © 1968 by Kodansha International Ltd. All rights reserved. Printed in Japan.

LCC 68–26558
ISBN 0–87011–070–5
JBC 0371–780696–2361

First edition, 1968
Third printing, 1976

Contents

Adaptor's Preface

A real city lay beyond the make-believe Edo of the ukiyo-e. In the prints, the inhabitants of old Edo move forever in a land of perpetual gaiety and beauty, but the men and women who lived in the real city must often have known poverty, disease, and crushing injustice. Only occasionally, in the ukiyo-e, is the brightly colored curtain drawn slightly aside—when a picture of a courtesan by Utamaro hints at degradation and physical decline, or when an actor-picture by Sharaku shows us the human weakness behind the histrionic mask.

With Harunobu, the illusion is never for a moment disturbed. His human figures are impersonal, remote, impossibly beautiful. By comparison, Sharaku's actors are monsters of realism, and Utamaro's beauties reek of the flesh. The backgrounds against which his lovely creatures are set call to mind, in their clear, bright colors, their clean-cut lines and their bold, easily recognizable indications of the seasons, some of the more colorful settings from the kabuki theater. Never did the cherry bloom more brightly, the autumn maples blaze more vividly, or the snow fall more prettily and pathetically than in this simplified and stylized world.

Yet the ukiyo-e, as much as the more festive scenes of the kabuki drama, was dealing with no remote past, no exotic land far from the Japan of the day, but with the actual, verifiable city in which its public lived. And since it was a popular art form, one can assume that this is how the masses of old Edo *wanted* to see it. Who, with the prints themselves before him, could blame them? Nevertheless, the more we of today are captivated by that exquisite never-never world, the more we wish that its artists had told us at least a little more about it as it really was.

The few photographs taken in the mid-nineteenth century, before the Meiji Restoration and the Westernization of the country, are not reassuring. Seen through a dark haze, the city looks somehow depressed. Even the few inhabitants of the Yoshiwara who found their way in front of the camera look sallow, surly, and (shades of Utamaro's slender beauties!) rather stunted. One hastens to restore a sense of proportion by recalling the murky indignities suffered at the hands of early cameramen by our own ancestors in the West. And at the same time one experiences the same mild frustration: why did the artists of the Edo period arouse our interest while failing to leave us a more complete picture of their city. Why did they refrain so absolutely from any moral comment on what they saw?

Perhaps this is to ask too much of a group of artists whose amiable purpose was, after all, solely to please. Yet this sin of omission—if so one can call it—can be laid at the door not only of the ukiyo-e, but of most Japanese painting as well. The middle-of-the-road tendency that is a feature of much of Japanese life seems to have affected the nation's art as well. On the one hand, with a few notable exceptions it displayed little taste for extravagant flights of imagination and remarkably little curiosity about worlds other than the human. Religious art, for example, eschewed both joyous profusions of cherubs and guilt-ridden visions of hell. The Buddhas and bodhisattvas of Japanese painting tend to be sedately decorative, and most of its mythological figures differ from the ordinary run of mortals only by a mild eccentricity.

On the other hand, Japanese art has seemed to feel no compulsion towards "truth" for its own sake, nor any compelling moral indignation; and it follows that it saw little point in satirizing or setting down in literal detail the less pleasing aspects of the world about it. It set about achieving its aims within a—superficially at least—less far-ranging world, a world less frightening, less ecstatic and, in one sense, more "human" than the world of Western art, with all the tensions and the restless drive engendered by its relentless dualisms of God and man, good and evil, justice and injustice. Thus, whether it aims to be profound, or whether—as in the ukiyo-e—it aims primarily to please, there is a certain consistent quality that distinguishes it from the art of the West.

In such circumstances, the ukiyo-e artists were obviously the last people of whom a faithful, non-idealized picture of their society could be expected. The fact remains that their artistic achievement was great, and that many of them went far beyond the cheap romanticism of the modern mass media, whose role their own in many ways resembled. Today, perhaps, we are less disposed to dismiss their work as merely decorative, and now that many of the assumptions that have impelled Western art are in question, our estimate of it may well be more favorable than at any time since Harunobu and his fellows first became known to the world in the last century.

J.B.

Harunobu and the Ukiyo-e

Suzuki Harunobu, who is believed to have been born in 1725 and to have died in 1770, was the originator of the Japanese polychrome print. He was, in addition, a great artist, the first in that astonishing gallery of figures that also included Kiyonaga, Utamaro, Hokusai, and a host of minor artists. With all these men, however, to write about their lives is to confess to varying degrees of ignorance. The situation is particularly unsatisfactory in Harunobu's case. There is none of the glamor of mystery, as with Sharaku. There is no body of anecdotes or other material—as with Hokusai—such as might lead one to attempt a portrait of the man. Nor are there any outstanding episodes comparable to the clash with the official censors that landed Utamaro in jail. Moreover, the period during which Harunobu produced his polychrome prints—which are our chief concern here, and which are incomparably better than anything he produced earlier—was short, and the prints themselves display a uniformity of style that leaves little room for discussion of development.

One can say something, however, about his position in history. Armed only with the knowledge that Harunobu was the first artist to produce polychrome prints, and encouraged by a certain simple, childlike quality in his work, one might be tempted to see him as a kind of primitive of the ukiyo-e. In fact, though, single-sheet prints had already been known in Japan for approximately a century at the time when Harunobu produced his first colored prints, and it is necessary for a true understanding of him to know something at least of the artists who went before, and of the social and historical background that produced the ukiyo-e print. Before presenting what little is known of Harunobu himself, therefore—and particularly since Harunobu is the earliest of the masters of the print who are dealt with in the present series—it seems appropriate here to give a short survey of that background.

The ukiyo-e print was a frail plant, reared in the hothouse of an economy secluded from the outside world for over two hundred years, and destined to fade and wither in the face of the chill blasts from outside that shook Japan in the nineteenth century. From that single fact spring many of its strengths and its limitations.

The development of maritime trade brought about by the use of the compass, and the discovery of new routes to the Far East, exerted an influence even on the distant islands of Japan. They brought Japan, in the age of Nobunaga and the early years of the Tokugawa regime—i.e. the end of the sixteenth and beginning of the seventeenth centuries—into direct contact with the culture of Europe, and made a not insignificant contribution to its industrial development. Yet from the time when the Tokugawa government issued its edict closing the country, all this came to an end. Most exchanges with foreign countries were cut off; any tendency for the Japanese to expand overseas was checked; and the import of foreign culture was drastically curtailed.

The losses to Japan thereby were very great, yet it meant at the same time that peace was to be preserved for long years at home, and that various domestic industries, protected from competition from abroad, were to show a steady growth. There were, it is true, some loopholes in the seclusion. The Chinese were allowed into Nagasaki harbor, and the Dutch were allowed to maintain a post on the island of Dejima through which trade was still possible. Artistically, this meant that Japan was not entirely cut off from the influence of the styles of China and the West; and the ukiyo-e print itself was, to a certain extent, influenced by the Chinese woodcut print and the Western etching. By and large, however, it grew and flourished with no incursions by alien strains, developing its own, exclusively Japanese, type of beauty and its own techniques. Ironically enough, the same beauty and the same techniques, after their heyday in Japan was past, were to exert a not inconsiderable influence on the art of the West.

The production of goods in Japan at the time was, of course, aimed solely at the domestic market. The flow of wealth was confined within the shores of Japan, and business capital was prevented from finding foreign outlets for its energies. Industry consisted mainly of handicrafts, and a large part of it was done in response to individual commissions. In time, however, the exchange of goods increased and a money economy evolved. This, together with the progressive division of labor between town and country and the rise of a merchant class, led in the Edo period to the growth of cottage industry and of handicrafts produced in workshops employing specialized artisans.

One example of the latter was the workshops of the *jihon-tonya*, the publishers of illustrated books. It was they—capitalists employing a varied collection of skilled artisans—who used their simple production techniques to manufacture the first ukiyo-e prints. These single-sheet prints were to cross the barriers of feudal domains and permeate every corner of the land, playing a role somewhat akin to that of modern journalism in the development of the Japanese people in the seventeenth and eighteenth centuries.

It was the *jihon-tonya* who supervised the activities of artist, engraver, and printer, as well as the distribution of the finished product. At his request, the artist—himself a kind of artisan, with a number of pupils of his own—would produce, with much pasting and altering, a draft picture. This was, first of all, submitted to the censor. There were various methods of censorship used at different periods, ranging from voluntary censorship by the publishers, through censorship by the heads of local districts, to censorship by an official censor.

The picture was next passed on to the engravers, who pasted copies of it onto the pieces of wood, usually carefully selected cherry wood, from which they carved the blocks—in the case of the polychrome print, one for the black outlines and several others for the colors. Their work, like that of the artist, involved a long apprenticeship, and an engraver was only allowed to do the more important parts of the pictures, such as the heads of human figures, after he had accumulated many years of experience.

The finished blocks would next go to the printers. Among the printers, too, there were various grades; the printers of color blocks, for example, looked down on those specialized only in black blocks. Before starting the printing proper, a "proof" would be made on special paper with the black block and sent to the artist, so that he could indicate the colors he required and make other specifications.

The tools used by the printer included, principally, large and small brushes for applying the ink and *baren*. The *baren*, a kind of round pad for smoothing the paper onto the block, included some made of twisted strands of bamboo leaves, others made of twisted strands of paper treated with astringent persimmon juice to toughen it, and others, made by twisting together iron wires, that were used only with gold and silver foil. The colors used were mainly vegetable; towards the end of the Tokugawa period pigments from the West began to be used, but they deprived the ukiyo-e of its characteristic flavor.

Works by the ukiyo-e artists themselves survive that depict the production and selling of ukiyo-e prints. For instance, there is a set of twin *ōban* polychrome prints by Utamaro in which the various stages in making a print are likened to the stages in the cultivation of crops, from the painting of the original picture (sowing the seed) to the distribution of the new print (autumn harvest). As one might expect, all the "farmers" in these scenes are beautiful women.

In the Tokugawa period, most of the *za* ("guilds"), organizations of artisans and merchants that had existed since the twelfth and thirteenth centuries, were replaced—with the exception of guilds directly run or controlled by the shogunate (gold and silver, copper, etc.) and those that sold articles (measures, seals, etc.) under the shogunate's direct supervision—by unions known as *kabu-nakama*, each of whose members had an official license *(kabu)* to carry on his trade. Their aim was to facilitate business and protect common interests; and they were convenient for the authorities too, since they promoted the healthy development of the economy, and made it easier to control the merchants. By such means, the members of the *jihon-tonya* organization were able to monopolize the business of selling prints. There were, in fact, other publishers, but they were treated as "undercover" dealers. In principle, the selling and leasing of licenses was unrestricted. A celebrated case of the use of this system was that of Tsutaya Jūzaburō, who bought up the *kabu* of two or three smaller enterprises and established what was to become perhaps the most important publishing house in the history of the ukiyo-e, the house that gave the world all the works of Sharaku and many of the best works of Utamaro.

Ukiyo-e, of course, included many paintings as well as prints. Very roughly speaking, the later ukiyo-e paintings were produced for the enjoyment of the comparatively affluent members of the merchant class by elderly ukiyo-e artists who had already established their reputations through their prints. Thus many of these paintings represent the artist at a stage when he was already past his prime (for a discussion of the ukiyo-e of the earliest days—specifically, the genre painting that was the spiritual predecessor of the ukiyo-e print—the reader is referred to the *Early Paintings* volume in the present series). The true development of the ukiyo-e took place as a type of handicraft, aimed at the general mass of the merchant class and undertaken on a commercial basis by a group of artisans who divided the labor, and among whom the artist was no more than a *primus inter pares*.

The nature of this merchant class had an important effect on the nature and development of the ukiyo-e itself. In medieval Europe, the titular ruler of a country in many cases had little control over the feudal lords under his suzerainty. His own lands were small, his incomes limited, his dignity and prestige negligible. In practice, a large number of local communities enjoyed something approaching complete independence. However, the development of industry, the strides made by commerce, the rise of the middle class, and the expansion of the towns provided the kings with natural allies in their struggle to consolidate their power. The greatest single phenomenon leading to the collapse of the feudal state is the development in the medieval towns of a moneyed class and the gradual accumulation of capital, together with the encroachment of wealth on the social preeminence hitherto enjoyed by rank and pedigree. The modern state became what it was thanks to the bourgeoisie. Class consciousness and awareness of class interests began to develop among the new bourgeoisie, and in particular among the merchants who were its chief representatives. Wealthy yet completely uneducated, both proud and stubborn, they gradually learned to apply their own cultivated attitudes and restricted knowledge to considering the problems of the day and their own position in particular.

The Tokugawa period in Japan saw a similar development of the towns, and a similar rise of a merchant class, with the result that in Japan, too, feudal wealth was gradually transformed into bourgeois wealth. The period that gave birth to the ukiyo-e was the period when the Japanese feudal system displayed its highest degree of organization, yet at the same time it was the period that saw its gradual collapse. Under the centralized rule of the Tokugawa shogunate and the blessed freedom from civil strife that it conferred on the nation, Japanese capitalism burgeoned and blossomed. The feudal lords, almost without exception, found themselves in increasing financial straits. With the fixed revenues provided by their territories, they were unable to keep up the extravagant double life necessitated by the need to keep residences both in their own fiefs and in Edo—where a shogunate jealous for the safety of its own rule required that they should spend part of their time. They tried various means to supplement their incomes, but eventually were driven, in most cases, to mortgage their incomes in return for loans from the merchants.

A large part of the tributes of rice exacted by the samurai class from the farmers went into the warehouses only to disappear again in payment of basic interest on borrowed capital. Thus the Japanese merchant class established its own power within the feudal organization, and used the power of its loaned capital to increase its own wealth further. The feudal lords, their finances squeezed dry by the new capitalist class, were forced eventually to put the screws on the people under their rule, and whatever they received in this way went, in turn, to line the pockets of the new capitalists.

The new merchant class made some attempt to formulate its own code to meet the needs of the new age—a "way of the merchant" as opposed to the old "way of the warrior." Yet despite this it failed, by and large, to escape from the narrow, feudalistic mentality and to develop any really positive outlook or way of life. For all the progress that capitalism was able to make in Japan, in the peaceful, stable atmosphere provided by the strong Tokugawa rule, it was still prevented by powerful feudal elements from developing in the direction it took in Europe. Unlike the merchants of Europe, and of England in particular, the merchants of Japan failed to progress beyond mere economic power and to make themselves the most powerful political authority in the state. Although, as someone said, "Let a wealthy merchant of Osaka show anger and all the lords of the land will quake in their boots," they were still, in just the same way as the peasants, under the thumb of the Tokugawa government and the Confucianist ideas of social status on which it based its rule. They failed, therefore, to secure from the old feudal regime adequate rights in respect of their own persons and property. The same men whose coffers were crammed with wealth, and to whom much of the brilliance of manners of the age must be attributed, were obliged to bow their heads to every petty retainer of the shogunate. Commercial capital, barred from developing outside the country, could not grow adequately, and wealth was frittered away in unproductive channels. The more successful, finding themselves despised and slighted despite their great riches and actual power, used their wealth to vie with each other in displays of stylishness and extravagance. The one place where they could find escape to freedom of a kind was the gay quarters. The habits of profligacy and extravagance that they developed spread eventually to the petty bourgeoisie also, and the philosophy of the typical Edoite, who "disdained to use money kept overnight," took shape.

Everything in their world was impermanent; nor was there anything particularly to live for save the passing pleasure. The gay quarters flourished, the geisha houses prospered. It was the momentary intoxication that made human life worthwhile. In matters of love, the unorthodox and the irregular won the day. As one writer at the time put it, "Life is but a dream, and who shall stay a hundred years? But a short way ahead lies darkness. What joy does the skeleton know? The only true pleasure is the pleasure of today."

The manners of the gay quarters began to determine those of ordinary society. Respectable wives and daughters, as the novelist Saikaku said in his *Diary of a Woman Who Loved Love*, "took over the ways of the prostitutes and the peculiar." The ordinary woman was obliged to take her cue from the harlot. Before long, society's "love of love" (or lust) gave rise to a drama and a graphic art on the same theme, and it was in this way that the ukiyo-e came into being: as a type of genre picture reflecting precisely these more frivolous aspects of the life of the merchant class.

The term ukiyo-e makes its first appearances in the 1780's, in the preface to an *ehon* ("picture book") by Hishikawa Moronobu entitled *Tsukinami no Asobi* (1682); in Saikaku's *The Woman Who Loved Love*, published in the same year; in the *Ukiyo-e Zoku Etsukushi*, also of the same year; and in the *Edo Kanoko* of 1684. It was a bourgeois art whose first exponent was a certain Hishikawa Kichibei, born in the province of Awa and better known as Hishikawa Moronobu, who had studied the official Kanō and Tosa schools of painting in his spare time. The *Edo Kanoko* mentioned above speaks of "Hishikawa Kichibei and Hishikawa Kichiemon of Sakai-machi Yokochō, ukiyo-e artists," while the *Edo Zukan Kōmoku* of 1689 has a section following that devoted to the Edokoro—the artists of the official Shogunate Bureau of Painting—entitled "Ukiyo-e Artists," in which it lists "Hishikawa Kichibei Moronobu of Tachibana-chō and his son Kichiemon Morofusa." The *Zōho Edo Sō Kanoko Meisho Taizen* of 1690 lists under the heading of "Yamato-e Artists" "Hishikawa Kichibei and Sakunojō of Muramatsu-chō 2-chōme," and the same names occur in another publication two years later. Whereas the artist connected with the Edokoro was an official painter, salaried and quite high in social status, the ukiyo-e painter was an artisan earning his living by piecework. One catered for the shogunate, the other for the new merchant class. One dealt chiefly in birds, flowers, landscapes, pictures of sages and famous personages of old, the other mostly with life in the gay quarters and the theaters. One dealt with the past and the world of fantasy, the other with scenes of actual life treated in a realistic fashion.

By depicting the life of the merchants, which neither the Kanō nor Tosa schools could touch, Moronobu did much to further the culture of his own class. He did a considerable number of paintings depicting life in the gay quarters and particular courtesans, some of them with a skillful blend of elements from both the Kanō and the Tosa schools. Nevertheless, his greatest achievement was undoubtedly in the field of the single-sheet print, which had its origins in the black-and-white illustrations found in books in earlier times.

It is not known exactly when Moronobu went to Edo, but it was probably in the Manji era, (1658–61), when he was already past forty. Edo had just been razed by two great fires, and with those fires the culture of the early Edo period, which had been largely a transplantation from the Kyoto-Osaka area, had perished. The greatest victim of the fires was the feudal ruling class, and it was the merchant class that benefited most as reconstruction work progressed. Already the merchants had begun to prosper, thanks to the continuing freedom from civil strife that the Tokugawa regime provided. They had begun to enjoy life and to acquire, in their own way, a taste for the arts; and the petty bourgeoisie who demanded some cheap, straightforward art suitable to their station in society found the answer—especially now, after repeated conflagrations—in cheap and easily available pictures.

Moronobu's prints must have sold like hot cakes. His work was handled by the *jihon-tonya* mentioned earlier, who, with their charmingly crude engraving techniques, now began to manufacture single-sheet prints for which Moronobu did the preliminary pictures. The result was a series of small works of art remarkable for their life, their sincerity and their liveliness.

The earliest of Moronobu's single-sheet black-and-white prints are believed to date from the Kambun era (1661–73). A set of twelve *ōban* prints, colored by hand in some copies and showing scenes of life in the Yoshiwara gay quarters, they have a certain crude vigor and freedom that remind one that, although the Tokugawa era had started, Japan was still not very far from the rougher and more vigorous age of the civil wars. Generally speaking, this type of print was sold either uncolored, or colored by hand. Occasionally the purchaser colored it himself, or he might get someone with artistic pretensions to color it for him. Some sets survive that include an appendix giving instructions for coloring.

Moronobu's women are not frail, as the women who appear in the ukiyo-e are often supposed to be. They are robust, and full of life. Yet already one notes in Moronobu's work the peculiar emphasis on the sexual element, and the characteristic view of women, that give the ukiyo-e such a special place in the history of

Japanese art. At the same time, its treatment of women, when compared with that of Western art, is typically Japanese; whatever their profession may have been, the women of the ukiyo-e are invariably withdrawn, elegant, graceful, and decorative.

It seems that the ukiyo-e artist in the time of Moronobu and his followers occupied a position somewhere between the artists of the Edokoro and the *hangi shita-e-shi* (the artisans who produced preliminary pictures for prints). As we have seen, the distinction between the Edokoro artists and the ukiyo-e artist was well-defined, but that between the ukiyo-e artist and the *hangi shita-e-shi* was not always so clear. A contemporary work, for example, classifies Moronobu and his eldest son as the former, and certain of Moronobu's pupils as the latter. Moronobu, of course, did preliminary designs for prints as well as painting as such. Possibly the *hangi shita-e-shi* were simply those ukiyo-e artists whose status in relation to their masters gave them a social standing a little lower than the rest.

The colors that came to predominate in the hand-colored prints of this period were vermilion *(tan)*, and yellow-brown *(suō)*, and the print itself was accordingly referred to as *tan-e*. The Hishikawa school, however, was fated not to carry its development very far. Following Moronobu's death, Moroshige gave promise of continuing the school, but the Hishikawa style died with his son (or pupil?) Moromasa. The popular artist who best represents the period of the *tan-e* is not a member of this school, but Torii Kiyonobu I. Kiyonobu's father, an Osaka actor, was also a proficient painter, and under the name of Torii Kiyomoto did theater posters for the theater at Dōtombori in Osaka. In 1687, he took his family to Edo, and in 1690 started doing posters for the Ichimura-za theater there. Unfortunately, none of his work has survived. Apart from the influence that he naturally absorbed from his father, Kiyonobu was attracted by the style of Moronobu, and also drew elements from the styles of the Kanō and Tosa schools, the official schools of painting. "From the end of the Genroku era," an old source says, "a kind of picture known as the *tan-e*, which used red and yellow to color prints, was put on sale; Kiyonobu and his son Kiyomasu were the most popular artists who did this type of picture. . . ."

Kiyonobu's prints use simple colors—red, yellow, green, and indigo—but the black line is unparalleled in its power and freedom. Although Hishikawa Moronobu also produced a fair number of paintings of kabuki, it was not until the Torii school that a really close connection developed between ukiyo-e and kabuki.

Kiyonobu's style was carried on by his sons and sons-in-law, the most notable of them being Kiyomasu. Just as the actor Ichikawa Danjūrō II, in the same period, gave a new refinement to the Ichikawa school of *aragoto* (violent, heroic acting) begun by Danjūrō I, so Kiyomasu perfected the style of the Torii school by giving new flexibility and brilliance to the strength and vigor of the actor-pictures started by his father. He is generally believed to have been Kiyonobu's eldest son, though he is sometimes said to have been his younger brother. One of the works he did in black with coloring added by hand is called *Shibaraku* (the name of a celebrated kabuki play), and shows Danjūrō II in a role he is known to have played at the Nakamura-za theater beginning in 1714.

A group of artists that produced a large number of brilliantly colorful paintings of courtesans in the early period of the ukiyo-e was headed by Kaigetsudō Ando, also known as Okazaki (or Okazawa) Genshichi. There are various theories as to when his work was produced, but it seems to have been around the same period as Kiyonobu. He was a resident of the Asakusa district of Edo, and, according to tradition, was banished to the island of Ōshima in 1714 as the result of a scandal involving a corrupt deal between an official merchant to the shogunate and a maid called Eshima in the shogun's private apartments. It is not known precisely why he was punished; the most interesting (and therefore, probably, the most suspect) theory is that he painted a pornographic picture for Eshima in return for aid in obtaining a shogunate order (he was a businessman himself).

What is more to the point is that he apparently had a house in Asakusa where he kept a number of pupils who produced a large number of brilliantly colored paintings in response to orders from rich patrons. The style of the school's paintings suggests the type of picture intended for framing, and it has been conjectured that Kaigetsudō's basic trade was painting *ema*, the "votive pictures" customarily commissioned for presentation to shrines. Whether this is true or not, it is a fact that the work of Kaigetsudō and of his pupils (or the men working for him in his shop; at least four have been identified) smacks strongly of commercial art. Of their prints, the whereabouts of only some twenty or so are known to us today. No signed specimens of Kaigetsudō's own work survive, but we know the names of many artists whose style obviously derives from his; they are mostly inferior in both color and line to the works attributed to Kaigetsudō and his immediate pupils.

Some authorities have dismissed Kaigetsudō's work as artistically worthless, and the faces of his women as vulgar. Others have criticized his stereotyped faces, the exaggerated variations in the thickness of his line, the lack of grace, and the general resemblance to poster art. Others, however, have pointed out that artists such as Miyagawa Chōshun, though superior to Kaigetsudō, owe much to him in their use of line (the clothes that Kaigetsudō's beautiful women wear are drawn with thick, springy lines, but the lines of their faces, hands, and feet are fine and soft) and in the postures of their female figures.

The ukiyo-e prints so far published had catered chiefly to the tastes of the petit bourgeois of Edo. From around the Kyōhō era (1716–36), however, there gradually appeared an increasing number of prints that made lavish use of a crimson pigment known as *beni* instead of the vermilion *(tan)* hitherto used, and also of prints that mixed glue with the black ink in order to produce a glossy luster similar to that of black lacquer. These are what are known as *beni-e* or *urushi-e* ("lacquer pictures").

The most notable of the artists who used this medium was Okumura Masanobu. The transition from Kiyonobu to Masanobu marks the disappearance of the "gourd-shaped" legs and thick, "snake-like" lines that were common hitherto, and a new emphasis on elegance and delicacy. In terms of the theater, it was a switch from the bold, rough, masculine *aragoto* style of acting to the more gentle and romantic *wagoto*. Masanobu's work included pictures both of prostitutes and of actors—especially the young actors, honored more for their boyish charms than the excellence of their art, who were known as *iroko*. He also did picture books. He showed a considerable professional pride, signing his works "Genuine work of Japanese artist Okumura Masanobu," and was himself in business as a publisher, having a shop where he published *beni-e* and popular illustrated novelettes. He was, in short, a typical merchant-cum-artist of an age in which the first stirrings of individualism were already perceptible. He is said to have died in either 1764 or 1768, at the age of seventy-eight.

According to eighteenth century sources, the merchants of Edo, who at the turn of the century had had at least some pretensions to being "gentlemen," had become thoroughly commercialized in their outlook by the second or third decade of the eighteenth century. The emphasis on hard cash and quick profits that became apparent in commerce as a whole also affected the ukiyo-e, and the quality of the hand-coloring in *beni-e* and *urushi-e* went down in inverse proportion to rising sales. A good example is the work of Okumura Toshinobu, said to have been either the son or the younger brother of Masanobu. Some copies of his work that survive in almost mint condition are clear evidence of how slapdash the hand-coloring was becoming in the face of the need for mass production. For precisely this reason, this method of coloring by hand was eventually to prove no match for color printing, and the simple *benizuri-e* was to prove a more effective way of meeting popular demand. The coloring of pictures by hand during this period seems to have been undertaken by a large number of semi-skilled employees who worked at the publisher's premises, and they could turn out as many as two hundred copies of the simpler *beni-e* in one day.

Although the single-sheet print is our main concern here, ukiyo-e work of considerable importance also appeared in the form of picture books, or of illustrations to the works of popular literature that enjoyed such a vogue in the eighteenth century. Thus the followers of Moronobu did illustrations for the popular historical or didactic tales known as *kanazōshi* and also the librettos of the popular *jōruri* ballads, while Kiyonobu did illustrations for many kabuki librettos and a few *jōruri* librettos. With the appearance of the so-called *kōzei-bon*—books of *jōruri*, fairy tales and the like with covers of richly decorated paper—the ukiyo-e artists began to do work for these, too, and their activity increased still further when the *kōzei-bon* gave way to the *akabon* ("red books," so called because of their vermilion covers) and *kurobon* ("black books"). Masanobu, already mentioned above, did a certain number of *akabon*, but a particularly large amount of work in this field was done by Kondō Kiyoharu. By trade a copyist, he is known for the characteristic "hammer-shaped" heads of his figures. Although his pictures lack tightness in their composition, they have an honest absence of affectation that somehow goes well with the fanciful, artless, naive tales they illustrate.

The most prolific artist in the field after Kiyoharu was Hanegawa Chinchō, who died in 1754. Slightly later than both Kiyoharu and Chinchō, and representing the transitional period from *akabon* to *kurobon*, is Nishimura Shigenaga. Said to have been a landowner who turned to book publishing, he developed a bland style that successfully covers up any traces of genius he may have had. However, his position in the history of the ukiyo-e is assured by the fact that he numbered among his pupils some of the greatest masters of the next generation, men such as Toyonobu, Harunobu, and Shigemasa. He died in 1756 at the age of fifty-nine.

The transition from the "red books" to the "black books" also marked a change in subject matter from innocent fantasies or moral tales to tales of martial prowess, biographies of famous heroes, legends associated with shrines and temples, tales of revenge, ghost stories, and so on. An artist especially famous for his work in this genre—apart from Kiyomitsu and other members of the Torii school, with whom we shall deal later—is Miyagawa Fusanobu. Not a great deal is known about his life except that he was originally a publisher who turned to doing illustrations when his business failed. The lives of most of these artists, in fact, are known to us only vaguely, but what we know is enough to show that it was difficult for an artist to make his living solely by doing the preliminary pictures for single-sheet prints, and that these works of popular literature were a vital source of income for all but the acknowledged masters who could rely on a steady stream of orders for their prints.

The books in question were not only sold in shops, but were also carried about the streets by vendors. A *hosoban* (size: 6 × 12 in.) print by Shigenaga shows a handsome youth dressed as a popular kabuki hero and carrying on his back a box with the legend "Books of Various Kinds." In medieval times, hawkers had been banned from time to time because they encroached on the privileges of the guild merchants, and similar measures were enacted in Tokugawa times also. In 1648, the shogunate started a system whereby only hawkers with an official badge were allowed to cry their wares, then in 1659 permits were given to persons over fifty or under fifteen, and to the disabled, as a measure to relieve the distress resulting from the recent great fire that had destroyed large areas of Edo. These regulations, however, do not seem to have been very strictly observed. Another extant picture shows a young boy who specialized in selling *beni-e*. On his back he carries a box labeled "Sophisticated Hand-Colored *Beni-e*" and surmounted by a model of a typical house in the gay quarters, while in his hand he holds a bamboo stick from which a *beni-e* is hung. This hawking of *beni-e* seems to have continued until the middle of the Kansei era (1789–1801). In 1721, various measures were taken to check the popularity of the ukiyo-e, including restrictions on their sale, but it seems to have had little effect in halting the steady development of the form.

The next important development in the ukiyo-e print was the gradual change-over to the application of color by block. Crude methods of printing in color had existed, of course, from early times, but it was not until sometime around the Enkyō and Kan'en eras (1744–51), it seems, that they were first applied to the single-sheet print. The block-printed *beni-e* that thus came to replace the hand-colored *beni-e* or *urushi-e* was known as *benizuri-e* ("red-printed picture"). Fenollosa, the American expert on Japanese art, who believed that the work of Okumura Masanobu provided a particularly sensitive indicator to changing fashions in the ukiyo-e from the Kyōhō era (1716–36) on, was of the opinion that a print by Masanobu showing a kabuki theater scene and dating from around 1741 was one of the last works done by any notable artist in the *urushi-e* style. According to tradition, it was in 1744 that an Edo publisher named Uemura Kichiemon devised the *kentō* system—a system of marking the blocks that makes accuracy in printing possible even when many blocks are used—and thereby paved the way for the great developments in color printing that lay just ahead. The same desire to experiment with new possibilities even led to the production, around the same period, of what were known as *mizu-e* ("water pictures"), prints exclusively using watercolors, with no black outlines at all.

Ukiyo-e artists who were active during the period of the *benizuri-e* include Nishimura Shigenaga and—already mentioned in connection with illustrations—Ishikawa Toyonobu. The latter in particular is noted for his romantic prints of courtesans—of which he produced large numbers even though he is traditionally said to have been a strict moralist who never himself so much as set foot inside the gay quarters. More important than either of these, however, are the members of the Torii school, among them Kiyonobu II, Kiyomitsu (died 1785), Kiyohiro (died 1776), Kiyoshige, and Kiyotsune. In the hands of this school of artists—which, as we have seen, was closely bound up with the theater from the very outset—the actor-picture made great strides.

It is fitting that the kabuki theater—that expression of the new awareness and the will to live of the rising merchant class—should have been a favorite theme of the early ukiyo-e artists, who portrayed its actors in the same simple colors as the courtesans of the gay quarters that were another focus of Edo merchant society. The pictures of actors, and especially the *iroko*, were extremely popular in an age in which homosexuality was common. They were also, however, eagerly sought after by the womenfolk of the merchant (and sometimes the samurai) class, who, unable to participate in the life of society outside the narrow confines of the home, had plenty of time for daydreaming, and seem to have been fascinated in equal measure by the effeminate airs of the young female impersonators and the grotesque blusterings of the players of villainous roles.

The theater and the gay quarters, thus, provided the early ukiyo-e with its twin themes, almost to the exclusion of any others. Technically, the ukiyo-e was developing steadily towards the polychrome print of which Harunobu was to be the first exponent. There was one master of the ukiyo-e however, who maintained a strictly intermediary position between the artists of the Edokoro—the official bureau of painting—and the print artists, restricting himself to paintings yet illustrating typical ukiyo-e themes. Miyagawa Chōshun, who died in 1752 at the age of seventy-one, is chiefly noted for the freshness of his coloring and for a style derived partly from the Tosa school of painting and partly from Hishikawa Moronobu, whom he much admired. One of his pupils was Miyagawa Shunsui, who used the surnames Miyagawa, Katsukawa, and Katsumiyagawa, and who is notable for having taught the great Katsukawa Shunshō. The reason why Chōshun disdained to do prints may have been that he aspired to a higher social status than was accorded the ukiyo-e print artist, or it may have been the limited opportunities for coloring that the *beni-e* and *benizuri-e* of his day offered. Either way, it was a loss to the ukiyo-e that an artist of such gifts should have set himself outside the mainstream of the ukiyo-e's development.

At this stage, the single-sheet ukiyo-e was still a special product of Edo, the great consumer city; the only ukiyo-e artist of note in the Kyoto-Osaka area was Nishikawa Sukenobu, who, according to the most plausible theory, died in 1751 at the age of eighty-one. He produced no single-sheet prints, but concentrated on picture books and paintings. Some consider his style—a style influenced by his studies of the Kanō and Tosa schools, by the Hishikawa school, and by certain painters of the Osaka-Kyoto area—as unexcelled in the field of ukiyo-e, while others find it monotonous and lacking in strength. Whichever view one accepts, it is a fact that he failed to establish any viable school of his own. More significant in the light of subsequent developments, however, are his interest in coloring and the fact that in his writings he declared his opposition to Chinese styles in art. Explicitly advocating a return to the native Yamato-e tradition, he emphasized the need for an artist to appeal to the human feelings rather than relying on mere technical proficiency. Although his followers were to include no great masters, his style was to have an enormous influence on that of Toyonobu, Harunobu, and other ukiyo-e artists in Edo.

In a sense, the Yamato-e was coming into its own once more. This style of painting, loosely embracing a number of characteristically Japanese attitudes to form, color, and emotional expression, enjoyed its heyday in the Heian (898–1185) and Kamakura (1185–1333) periods only to be overwhelmed during the ensuing feudal period by the Chinese styles favored by the ruling samurai class. The early ukiyo-e paintings were essentially a continuation of the same tradition, now out of the hands of the debilitated official schools of Yamato-e, but this new growth was stifled in the early Tokugawa period. It gradually emerged again, however, as the new merchant class began to develop its own culture, and achieved its full flowering with the masters of the polychrome prints. Thus although the merchant class failed to develop any philosophy of its own to replace the Confucianism of the samurai class, it did develop its own, in a sense more Japanese, culture. In the way it harks back to the traditions of the Yamato-e, the ukiyo-e can be seen as one of those periodic returns—here, of course mainly unconscious—to things Japanese that always seem to follow a period of overwhelming foreign influence, and is complementary to the more explicit movement toward a revival of Japanese studies that occurred in the world of scholarship.

As we have already seen, efforts were made in the Kyōhō era (1716–36), during the rule of Yoshimune, the eighth Tokugawa shogun, to check the growth of the ukiyo-e print. Various short-sighted attempts were made, in the name of frugality and the checking of corruption, to reduce the amount of money spent on pleasure, including the use of extravagant materials in the manufacture of prints. A number of works—among them some of Sukenobu's picture books—were actually banned and the blocks destroyed, though it is extremely difficult to see why some of them, at least, should have been considered at all detrimental to public morals.

These efforts were doomed to failure, partly because of the laxity of the government itself. Corruption within official circles spread, and it was during the Meiwa and An'ei eras (1764–81)—a period symbolized by Tanuma Okitsugu, a powerful politician who eventually became the shogun's chief minister and was noted for the corruption and decadence of his administration—that the ukiyo-e underwent some of its most remarkable developments. It was in this period, in fact, that the color print, in which the number of colors used had gradually been increasing, emerged as the *nishiki-e*—the true polychrome print using ten or more blocks, with additional, subtle color effects achieved by overprinting.

Some idea of the temper of the times is given by a work published in 1776, which declares: "men sell their weapons and their saddles for money to spend on pleasure. The hand that should grasp the sword holds a slender cane of sandalwood; the man who should be skilled at handling his horse is expert only in the ways of pleasure boats and palanquins . . . the swords by his side are as slender as the pokers of a charcoal brazier." "The common people," another work says, "acquire wealth without labor and accumulate riches without effort. In the morning, another's riches come drifting into one's own pocket; in the evening, one's own fly off into another's hands. There is no idea of frugality or of saving, even for a brief while. The money is spent in the gay quarters, at the theater, or in gratifying the gullet at stylish restaurants; today's wealth is tomorrow's poverty. . . ."

It was in such an age that the simple *benizuri-e* gave way to the brilliant *nishiki-e*. "Long ago, when I was a lad," says another work published in 1776, "the 'Edo picture' [the ukiyo-e] portrayed Ichikawa Danjūrō, Ōtani Hiroji, and other actors in simple black with a lacquer-like gloss; it was a very rustic affair, little better than the Ōtsu-e [a crude type of picture made at Ōtsu, not far from Kyoto, for travelers to take home with them as souvenirs]. But the Edo picture today is an infinitely stylish and colorful affair, and impresses in a way that even the ukiyo-e of Nishi-kawa Sukenobu could never do."

The second year of the Meiwa era, 1765, was a significant date. The shogunate, following the advice of its finance minister, Lord Kawai of Echizen, made another attempt to reform the economy by taking steps towards a reform of the monetary system. Another of the mainly ineffective sumptuary edicts had been issued the previous year. In a number of the poorer provinces, peasant risings were occurring. And it was in this same year that Suzuki Harunobu, a gifted artist, who during the past decade had been producing mostly *benizuri-e*, embarked on the production of polychrome prints.

Unlike the *benizuri-e*, the polychrome print did not come into being as a commodity aimed at the masses, but was commissioned by a group of leisured and wealthy merchants and samurai in Edo. Unlike the *benizuri-e*, again, it was printed on the best-quality paper, using costly pigments and employing all the refinements of the engraver's and printer's art, including *karazuri* (embossing on white paper for a three-dimensional effect) and *kime-dashi* (a special effect of texture taking advantage of the natural grain of the wood). It was this sumptuousness, together with the brilliance of its coloring, that earned it the name of *nishiki-e* ("brocade picture").

The first *nishiki-e* took the form of "picture calendars," in which the number of days in, and the arrangement of, the months during the coming year were incorporated in various ingenious ways into the design of the picture. The men who commissioned them were amateurs of literature and the arts dwelling in that section of society where the upper-class merchants tended to mingle with members of the ruling samurai class. Such men frequently formed societies devoted to the composing of *haiku* and the appreciation of the arts in general, and one of their many elegant pastimes was the exchange of picture calendars at the New Year, each member vying with the rest in the elaborateness and ingenuity of his offerings. It was one of these same societies, known as Kyosen-ren ("Kyosen Group") because it was led by a man whose artistic pseudonymn was Kyosen, that commissioned Harunobu's first set of *nishiki-e* prints, the *Zashiki Hakkei* ("Eight Views of Indoor Life"; see Pls. 14–21), for which the basic idea was supplied by Kyosen himself.

At this early stage, a set of *nishiki-e* was often sold in a box, or in an elaborately decorated folder of paper; not infrequently, these bore not only the name of the artist responsible, but also those of the engraver and the person responsible for the original concept. In other cases, the names of artist, engraver, and printer were set alongside each other. As this clearly shows, each work was thought of by its publisher as a combination of fine and decorative art in which several people cooperated to produce something as near perfect in every detail as possible, regardless of the expense. Thus the first edition of the eight prints of the *Zashiki Hakkei* came in a fine box of paulownia wood. It sold, moreover, for a sum of money that put it beyond the means of the peasants, artisans, and minor merchants who bought the cheaper ukiyo-e, and clearly marked it as a luxury item intended for the wealthy merchants or samurai. Before long, however, the custom of recording the engraver's and printer's names was abandoned. Later works were obviously produced more cheaply, and for a wider market. Even the *Zashiki Hakkei* exists in a later edition in which the colors have become brighter and the signature of Harunobu himself replaces that of Kyosen, which appears on the earlier version. It is clear, in short, that the *nishiki-e* was too attractive to remain for long in the hands of a few wealthy dilettanti.

Unlike many other ukiyo-e artists, Harunobu was born a true son of Edo, though there are differing theories as to the precise district in which he lived. His real family name was Hozumi, his given name Jihei, and he also used the elegant pseudonymns Chōeiken and Shikojin. He is said to have been a pupil of Nishimura Shigenaga (or, others say, of Nishikawa Sukenobu), though in his pre-*nishiki-e* days, he produced a series of pictures of kabuki actors that clearly show the influence of the Torii school. It has also been suggested that his style was influenced by the painting of Ming dynasty China, and that his graceful, willowy figures have their origin in imported copies of the colorful works of, for example, Ch'iu Ying (fl. 1540). Besides actor pictures, he also did, during his early period, a number of pictures of beautiful women and children, and some *mitate-e* (classical themes in contemporary guise; "parodies"). Yet from the whole of this early period, which dates from 1754 to 1765, only some forty or fifty prints and a number of picture books are known to us; this is a far smaller output than the six hundred prints or more that he produced during the five years of his *nishiki-e* period, and the early prints themselves give little hint of the maturity that he was to achieve so suddenly when he turned to full-color works. He died in 1770 at the age of forty-five, though various authorities have put his age at forty-seven, fifty-three, or sixty-seven.

Almost without exception, the subjects of Harunobu's *nishiki-e* are human figures, usually shown in pairs. They cover a fairly large range of types, from famous women of ancient times such as Murasaki Shikibu, the author of the *Tale of Genji*, to contemporary matrons, young girls, prostitutes, teahouse waitresses, geisha, young men and children. His special favorites, however, were two young women celebrated throughout Edo at the time for their great beauty. One of them was "Kasamori" Osen, the daughter of the proprietor of a teahouse that stood in the grounds of the Kasamori Shrine. The other was Ofuji, daughter of the owner of a shop selling toothpicks that stood behind the temple of Kannon in the Asakusa district. The two of them were frequently mentioned in the popular literature of the day, and it is said that people would come from far and wide just to get a glimpse of them. It was the fashionable thing to compare their charms in pictures or in prose, and in the contemporary equivalent of a modern beauty contest Osen was chosen as a kind of "Miss Edo" of the day.

Harunobu's prints also include a considerable number of domestic scenes in which young married women are shown with their children. One print, even, shows a bespectacled grandmother as well—a rarity, indeed, in the ukiyo-e. The number of prints depicting children increases towards the end of Harunobu's career. Certain features of these prints—such as the prevalence of sturdy male children matched with young and attractive matrons in various states of dishabille (Pl. 27, for example), together with some works that obviously have a mildly salacious touch (Pl. 4)—remind one that in the ukiyo-e, of all genres, "innocence" is not always to be taken at its face value. Yet even so, it seems clear that Harunobu had a genuine affection for children, and he was especially skillful with scenes showing them at play.

There is no individuality whatsoever in the faces of Harunobu's figures. They are childlike and delicate, with a remote, withdrawn quality that somehow recalls the world of the famous *Tale of Genji Picture Scroll* of the twelfth century. There is little facial distinction made between the sexes, even. A non-Japanese unfamiliar with the conventions of Japanese dress and hairstyles might be excused for not even noticing, in many cases, that one of the figures in a particular print is a man. If he knows his kabuki, however, he will already be aware that on the stage an epicene appearance and mincing manner were the hallmarks of the romantic hero, of the gallant of the gay quarters. So it was in the ukiyo-e: among the men portrayed, only the aged and unattractive wore their masculinity, as it were, on their sleeve.

One further characteristic of Harunobu's themes that should be noted is his fondness, shared with most other ukiyo-e artists, for *mitate-e*—the pictures, and especially the sets of prints, showing "classical themes brought up to date." Along with these, one should classify the prints that include a classical poem, which they are supposed to illustrate. In both cases, of course, one of the aims is simply to provide a pretext, a framework for a series of changes rung on the familiar themes of beautiful women, beautiful clothes, and the shifting seasons. At the same time, however, they indubitably served to set the ukiyo-e—this upstart merchant class art—within the context of a tradition, the tradition of Japanese literature and the Yamato-e. How far this was conscious, how far an unconscious reaction against the atmosphere of Chinese, Confucianist learning imposed by the ruling class, it is impossible to estimate.

It is remarkable how, within the comparatively narrow range of his themes, Harunobu avoids monotony. Much of his success here is attributable to the wonderful skill of his backgrounds, which suggest with unerring simplicity and great freshness the changing seasons, day and night, and the various aspects of the Japanese interior.

The great majority of Harunobu's prints are in the *chūban* (8 × 11 in.) size, that is, almost square. This size seemed to suit his style particularly well; although there are a few *ōban* (10 × 15 in.) and *hashira-e* ("pillar pictures," which are very tall in relation to their width), he seems not to have been at home with them. In composing his scenes—often with an oblique perspective that, again, recalls the world of the *Tale of Genji* scroll—Harunobu showed an enormous skill without achieving the daring of Utamaro's later work or the classical balance and proportion of Kiyonaga's groups. His colors—which became gayer as his *nishiki-e* period progressed—are fresh and bright. They may not have the dignity of the coloring in Kiyonaga's work, or the subtlety of that of Utamaro, yet they combine with the sweetness and simplicity of the human figures to produce something that neither Kiyonaga nor Utamaro have—an ineffable, fresh, otherworldly, almost fairy-tale quality that is quite unique, and that forbids any tendency to treat Harunobu as a kind of "primitive" of the *nishiki-e*.

As already suggested, to speak of "innocence" in Harunobu is to use the term in a relative sense. The ukiyo-e was, after all, the product of an introverted, decadent society, and like the popular literature of its day it was adept at innuendo. For this reason, one may well prefer Harunobu's pictures of courtesans—which, paradoxically, seem to attain an almost Buddhist sense of unworldliness and detachment—to his pictures of "chaste" young matrons dandling their male infants, which somehow give a foretaste of the more decadent later ukiyo-e. For similar reasons, one may prefer the prints that illustrate simply some straightforward theme to those that indulge in tortuous references to literature or in the rather decadent fancifulness so typical of the age. How the individual reacts to particular works will depend on his own temperament. Yet it remains true that even in the most "doubtful" of Harunobu's works there is a childlike, innocent quality that is quite lacking in the work of, say, Utamaro, with its faint yet all-pervasive odor of sensuality. This is true even of Harunobu's many pornographic works, which retain a freshness and simplicity (the human beings, both male and female, are exactly the same fairy-tale creatures that occur in his non-erotic works) that make their grosser aspects seem somehow out of place.

Harunobu has been referred to as an artist of youth and the spring, but it might be truer to call him an artist of the passing spring. One senses in his work a mild regret and a faint nostalgia that somehow accord ill with the image of youth and

26

vigor. It is not to decry the artistic value of his prints to point out that they are in some ways symbolic of the more morbid, passive side of Edo period culture. In the West, it was at a very similar moment in history—when the life of religious retreat had begun to lose its appeal, when the world to come had begun to recede in the face of the promise of the here-and-now, and when man's spiritual center of gravity had shifted to the present life—that there occurred a mighty awakening of the individual and of a new, rational, critical spirit. In Japan, too, the promise of a life of peace beyond the grave was ceasing to offer man's only prospect of escape from the round of suffering, and he was beginning, as in the West, to taste for the first time the joys that make life worth living. But in Japan his reaction was to steep himself in pleasure and fantasy that was as far removed from true rationality and individualism as anything that had gone before.

The beautiful women that Harunobu saw about him were real flesh and blood; yet in the act of portraying them his art grew wings and, like some frail, many-colored butterfly, was borne off into a delicate, remote realm of frivolity and fantasy where it remained, playing eternally, untroubled by the cold blasts of reality.

Japanese Titles of the Prints

There are no generally accepted English titles for the prints reproduced in the following pages, even for those that have already appeared in other works in English. Moreover, many titles contain literary and other allusions that cannot be conveyed simply in English, which means that the translations are inevitably only approximate. This, together with the family resemblance that so many ukiyo-e titles bear to each other, adds still further to the difficulty of identifying a particular print or series. The only sure means of identification is the original Japanese title. For the benefit of the reader who wishes to investigate further, a list of the Japanese titles for the prints reproduced in this volume is appended below. It should be noted, however, that in some cases even these are no more than descriptions of the works attached to them by later scholars, the original titles being unknown to us today.

1. Saru-hiki
2. Kakujō no Yūjo
3. Sagi Musume
4. Hata-ori
5. Tomiyoshi-ya Mae
6. Shimizu from "Fūryū Nana-Komachi Yatsushi"
7–8. Sekidera and Amakoi from "Fūryū Yatsushi Nana-Komachi"
9–10. Ōmu and Sōshi-Arai from "Fūryū Yatsushi Nana-Komachi"
11–12. Kayoi and Sotoba from "Fūryū Yatsushi Nana-Komachi"
13. Mitate Chikurin Shichi-Kenjin
14. Ōgi no Seiran from "Zashiki Hakkei"
15. Daisu no Yau from "Zashiki Hakkei"
16. Kyōdai no Shūgetsu from "Zashiki Hakkei"
17. Kotoji no Rakugan from "Zashiki Hakkei"
18. Antō no Sekishō from "Zashiki Hakkei"
19. Tenugui-kake no Kihan from "Zashiki Hakkei"

THE PLATES

1. "The Performing Monkey" ◆ *chūban*
◆ Tetsuo Aoki Collection

"Dances" by performing monkeys were popular from the Kamakura period on, as entertainment and as magic to ward off disease. At one time, there were as many as six professional showmen with monkeys in Kyoto. In this work the monkey trainer is idealized as a beautiful young woman whose monkey is performing an auspicious dance known as Sambasō. The treatment of the background is most unusual for an ukiyo-e print.

33

2. "Courtesan Riding on a Crane" ♦ *chūban* ♦ Seiichirō Takahashi Collection

Like other ukiyo-e artists, Harunobu did various prints in which the supernatural beings of Chinese mythology are shown as beautiful women in contemporary dress. The courtesan here shown seated on the back of a crane in flight, reading a lengthy love letter, could refer to either of two figures in classical Chinese literature. Harunobu also did a picture calendar showing a beautiful woman riding on a wild goose, and another showing a woman on a bird resembling a phoenix.

34

3. "Heron Maiden" ◆ *chūban* ◆ Private collection
This print clearly alludes to the classical dance known as "Heron Maiden," which is accompanied by a ballad that refers to "the heron standing forlorn in the lightly falling snow of eventide." First performed in the Hōreki era (1753–59), the dance was taken up by various famous actors. It was revived in Meiji times, doubtless with many alterations, yet the first glimpse of the dancer as the curtain goes up is still strongly reminiscent of the figure in this print.

4. "At the Loom" ◆ *chūban* ◆ Atami Art Museum
    This print has a sense of movement unusual in Harunobu's work. The coloring, though simple, is extremely effective against the crimson background, and skillful use is made of *karazuri* (blind stamping resulting in an embossed effect). The small boy with his tongue sticking out who is lifting the hem of the young woman's kimono gives an oddly salacious touch to what seems at first glance a characteristically innocent work.

5. "Outside the Entrance to Tomiyoshiya"
◆ *hosoban* ◆ *benizuri-e* ◆ Private collection
   Another print with almost the same composition as this, a *nishiki-e* in the series "Eight Views of Indoor Life," is shown in Plate 14. The chief differences here are the short curtain bearing the name "Tomiyoshiya" (doubtless that of a house in the gay quarters) that hangs above the latticework, and the absence of the fan that one of the young women holds in the later work. This is a particularly fine specimen of the comparatively few works surviving from Harunobu's pre-*nishiki-e* period.

6. "Shimizu" from "The Seven Komachis in Modern Style" ◆ *hosoban* ◆ Private collection

This series is inspired by seven famous episodes associated with the Heian period poetess and beauty, Ono no Komachi. The theme is a favorite with ukiyo-e artists, but the relationship between the original episodes and the actual pictures is often rather obscure. The original story here, for example, concerns a visit by Komachi to the Kiyomizu Temple and her unexpected meeting there with the priest Sōjō Henjō, but apart from the poem and a picture of the temple in the inset, there is little to link the print with this episode.

38

7–8. "Praying for Rain" and "Sekidera Temple" from "The Seven Komachis in Modern Style" ◆ *hosoban* ◆ Private collection

A poem praying for rain and a picture of an umbrella in the inset of the lefthand print are fairly obvious references to the title. In the picture itself, the younger woman is using her pipe to draw the toy boat towards her. The Sekidera Temple of the righthand print is the temple where Komachi, as an old woman of over one hundred, is said to have dragged out her wretched last days. The only connection between Komachi and the buxom wench shown here would seem to be the suggestion of rusticity and poverty.

39

9-10. "Parrot" and "Washing the Manuscript" from "The Seven Komachis in Modern Style" ◆ *hosoban* ◆ Private collection

The "parrot" of the lefthand print—illustrated literally in the painting on the screen in the picture—is a reference to an episode of Komachi's old age, when her reply to a sympathetic verse sent her by the emperor was the emperor's own verse with only one syllable changed. Char-

acteristically, Harunobu writes the word *ōmu* (parrot) with characters meaning "a dream of meeting." The righthand print is a reference to an episode in which a courtier accused Komachi of stealing a poem from the *Manyōshū* anthology. When he produced a *Manyōshū* manuscript including the poem as proof of his charge, Komachi dipped the manuscript in water to prove that he himself had recently written in the poem in question.

11–12. "The Regular Visitor" and "Sotoba" from "The Seven Komachis in Modern Style" ♦ *hosoban* ♦ Private collection

The lefthand print is suggested by the story of the young man to whom Komachi promised herself if he would only visit her house for one hundred nights in succession—and who died on the ninety-ninth night. The inset has a picture of a typical young man of Harunobu's day on his way to the gay quarters, while the print proper shows a courtesan standing on the veranda while her young attendant calculates on her fingers the number of visits paid to her by a regular patron. The Sotoba episode tells how Komachi in her old age sat down on a gravestone to rest and was rebuked by a priest. Here, a lusty countrywoman carrying firewood is resting on a tree stump while her young son throws a stone at something in a nearby tree.

41

13. "The Seven Sages of the Bamboo Grove in Modern Guise" ◆ transverse *ōban* ◆ *benizuri-e* Tokyo National Museum

This work is suggested by the seven legendary wise men of ancient China who, disgusted with the world, retired into the remote mountains where they would gather in a bamboo grove to discuss philosophy and enjoy each other's company. To represent such men by a group of prostitutes might seem rather inappropriate, even

賢人も
志やれ乃
浮世や
君
お
春

画工 鈴木春信

in an ukiyo-e, but one should remember that the
sages in question are traditionally said to have
been fond of tippling and to have been willing,
even, to play on the lute if requested.

43

14. "Hazy Morning Sunlight Suggested by a Fan" from "Eight Views of Indoor Life" ◆ *chūban* ◆ Private collection

The "Eight Views" of Hsiao-hsiang, each of them associated with a particular time of day or year, were celebrated in Chinese painting and verse from early times. In this set, Harunobu applies this conventional framework very loosely, taking eight everyday scenes and relating them, not to specific places, but to the atmospheric or seasonal conditions conventionally associated with each of the eight places celebrated in such sets. In this print, a young courtesan is seen returning home in the morning, using her fan to shelter her from the hazy sunlight.

44

15. "Night Rain Suggested by a Tea Stand" from "Eight Views of Indoor Life" ◆ *chūban* ◆ Private collection

In this print, the sound of the water bubbling in the kettle on the lower shelf of the tea-making stand is compared to that of "night rain" in the original series. Lulled by the sound, a young woman dozes, while a mischievous small boy ties a long strip of paper to her hair and another young woman watches in amusement. Note the skillful placing of the three figures in relation to the composition as a whole.

16. "The Autumn Moon Suggested by a Mirror" from "Eight Views of Indoor Life" ◆ *chūban* ◆ Private collection

The relationship between the moon and the mirror on its stand is fairly obvious—at least to anyone used to the devious minds of the ukiyo-e artists. The pampas grass visible outside the window is a sure sign that it is autumn. One could find various other literary references if one wished—for example, in the pattern of the kimono worn by the young girl whose hair is being done up by the older woman— but such relationships are tenuous at best, and add little to our enjoyment today.

17. "Wild Geese Alighting Suggested by a Koto" from "Eight Views of Indoor Life" ◆ *chūban* ◆ Private collection

The *koto* (Japanese lute) shown here is of the thirteen-stringed variety known as *tsukushi-goto*. One of the young women is fitting the plectrum on her finger, while the other holds a book entitled *Collection of Koto Music*. In the garden, the autumn *hagi* (bush clover) is in bloom— a sign that it is also the season for wild geese to come flying across the sky. The intention is doubtless to compare the sound of the *koto* with the cry of the wild geese.

47

18. "Sunset Suggested by a Lantern" from "Eight
Views of Indoor Life" ◆ *chūban* ◆ Private collection

Outside, the darkness is still not deep enough to
obscure the stream and the maple tree in the garden,
but indoors it is growing dusky, and one young woman is lighting a lantern for another who is intent
on the letter she is reading.

48

19. "Homing Sailboats Suggested by a Towel Stand" from "Eight Views of Indoor Life" ◆ *chūban* ◆ Private collection

The young woman who has been lying dozing in the room beyond the veranda is washing her hands, while her companion placidly continues her sewing. The towel hung to dry on the stand in the foreground is likened to the sails of the boats returning home over the lake that are conventionally shown in one of the "eight views" of the series.

20. "The Evening Bell Suggested by a Clock" from
"Eight Views of Indoor Life" ◆ *chūban* ◆ Private
collection

The great bell of the temple by the lake, whose
tolling at eventide is heard drifting over the waters

in one of the original eight views, is here reduced to
the bell of a clock. One of the young women on the
veranda is listening to it; the other, judging from
her dress, has probably just come from the bath and
seems still to be drying herself.

21. "Snow in the Dusk Suggested by a Black Lacquered Container" from "Eight Views of Indoor
Life" ◆ *chūban* ◆ Private collection

A young girl is stretching silk floss over a round,
black lacquered box—which is supposed to suggest

the snow-covered landscape at dusk that forms one
of the original set of landscapes. The room shown
has, perhaps, a rather chilly, desolate air, but the conceit, even so, must seem rather farfetched to the
modern mind.

22. "Yūgao in Modern Guise" ◆ *chūban* diptych ◆
Tokyo National Museum

This work is suggested by the celebrated "Yūgao"
chapter in the *Tale of Genji*. The original relates how
Genji is on his way to visit his old nurse, who is sick,
when his attention is captured by a white moon-
flower growing over the eaves of a shabby, tumble-
down building. He orders a retainer to fetch one for
him. The retainer enters the gate and breaks off a
flower, whereupon a door opens and an odd-looking
maidservant appears. She beckons him, and gives him
a white fan impregnated with incense, bidding him

bear the flower to Genji on it. The flowers and the rustic gateway are visible in this print, but the fan bears not a flower but a love letter. The man, too, has his fan open, while the child attendant carries an insect cage—details whose relevance to the original "Yūgao" is not immediately apparent.

千鳥の玉川 陸奥前底津
夕されは
汐風こして
野田の
たま川
ちとり鳴也

23. "The Tamagawa with Plovers" from "The Six Tamagawas" ◆ *chūban* ◆ Tokyo National Museum

The "Six Tamagawas"—six rivers or streams in various parts of Japan, all bearing the name Tamagawa ("Jewel River")—were a favorite theme of ukiyo-e artists, and at least three series by Harunobu are known, two in *chūban* and one in *hashira-e* size. The *chūban* set represented here includes a poem in an inset on each print. The poem in this example includes a reference to "The Tamagawa at Noda, where the plovers cry. . . ."

24–25. "The Tamagawa at Kōya" and "The Tamagawa with Bush Clover" from "The Six Tamagawas in Contemporary Scenes" ◆ *hashira-e* ◆ Tokyo National Museum

These are two prints from another of Harunobu's "Six Tamagawas" series. The Tamagawa of the first print is a small stream near a temple of the great monastery on Mt. Kōya, and the young woman carries the bamboo basket-hat and flute of the itinerant monk. In the second, Harunobu was probably inspired by a poem about bush clover (*hagi*) blooming beside a stream in which the autumn moon is reflected; it is doubtless the reflection of the moon that the young woman in the print is gazing at so intently.

55

28. "Two Young Women Reading a Letter" ◆
chūban ◆ Takaharu Mitsui Collection

This is a fine example of the techniques of the *nishiki-e*. The effective colors—for instance, the contrast between the purple outer garment worn by the courtesan and the white garment worn by her companion—may have been chosen by Harunobu himself, but it was the printer who made such skillful use of embossing and the natural grain of the paper in the treatment of the white robe. Although such techniques belong, strictly speaking, to the realm of decorative art, they did much to give variety to the essentially two-dimensional woodblock print.

31-
ty i
Tal
tior

T
kno
firs
qua
ma
of
inti
seco
ing
sno
by

29. "Cat's Cradles" ◆ *chūban* ◆ Tokyo National Museum

A charming scene in which two young women are seen absorbed in their task of making cat's cradles. It is winter, and their legs are hidden beneath the quilt that covers the *kotatsu*. The mere presence of a *kotatsu*—a kind of footwarmer using a sunken charcoal brazier surmounted by a wooden frame over which a quilt is placed—gives the scene an added sense of warmth and intimacy for any Japanese.

いせのうみにちゞれしるらんいまこそはかひあるべき

権中納言敦忠

37. "Gon Chūnagon Atsutada" ◆ *chūban* ◆ Takaharu Mitsui Collection
    The poem by Atsutada, which appears in the
Gosen Wakashū anthology, compiled in the early
tenth century, depends in part on an untranslatable
pun. However, it is not essential to the enjoyment
of the picture itself, which is typical of Harunobu
in its idealization of the diving woman—an interesting contrast to the strong sensuality with which
Utamaro, for example, treats the same subject.

38. "Chūnagon Tomotada" ◆ *chūban* ◆ Atami Art Museum

The poem sings of the pain of not meeting a loved one, and the connection between poem and picture is obviously formed by the love letter that one of the women holds. However, the picture is also clearly intended to suggest Han-shan and Chih-teh, two eccentrics who frequently occur in Zen art. Chih-teh, who did cleaning and other menial tasks at a Chinese monastery, is usually shown holding a broom, while Han-shan, a beggar to whom Chih-teh gave leftover food, is shown with a sutra scroll—transformed in this print into the love letter.

39. "Kino Tomonori" ◆ *chūban* ◆ Takaharu Mitsui Collection

"At eventide," runs the poem, "comes the cry of the plover who has lost his mate in the mist that creeps along the banks of the river Saho." The poem is skill-fully echoed in Harunobu's print, with its hooded beauty who turns her head, startled by the cry of the birds as she walks along the river bank with her child attendant. In such a context, the "lost mate" of the poem acquires a new, more human significance.

68

風をいたみ
岩うつ
浪の
をのれのみ
くだけて
ものを
われも
ころが

源重之

鈴木春信画

40. "Minamoto Shigeyuki" ◆ *chūban* ◆ Private collection

The poem, from the celebrated *Hyakunin Isshu* anthology, likens the gale-swept waves breaking over the rocks to the turbulent emotions filling the poet's own lovelorn heart. It is hardly matched by Harunobu's print. Despite the attempt to suggest a strong wind, and the skillful use of *karazuri* in depicting the waves, the work scarcely disturbs the surface of the serenity characteristic of all his prints.

41. "Sosei Hōshi" ◆ *chūban* ◆ Takaharu Mitsui Collection

"As far as the eye can see," says the poem, "there is nothing but willow trees and cherry blossoms, their colors mingling till the capital seems a very pattern of spring brocade." In the print, too, it is spring, and two young women stand at the entrance to a shrine overlooking the city of Kyoto.

70

42. "Gon Chūnagon Sadaie" ◆ *chūban* ◆ Takaharu Mitsui Collection

This print has a subdued, almost melancholy quality that contrasts sharply with the brilliance of that shown in Plate 41. "As far as the eye can see"—the poem begins with the same phrase—"there is neither spring blossom nor autumn maple, nothing but the autumn twilight and a rude thatched hut by the bay." The poem is well known, and is sometimes quoted as an expression of the Zen spirit, although the poet lived long before Zen was introduced into Japan.

71

43. "The Potted Trees in Modern Guise" ◇ *chūban* ◈ Atami Art Museum

The origin of this print is a well-known story, first found in the martial epic *Taiheiki* and the history *Masu-kagami* and later made the subject of a Nō play and various puppet dramas and kabuki plays. The episode illustrated in "modern guise" here tells how the Shogun Tokiyori, who has become a monk, is caught in the snow and is given shelter by Tsuneyo, a samurai in straitened circumstances, who chops up his three cherished miniature trees—a plum, a cherry, and a pine—in order to make a fire for him.

44. "Kasamori Osen" ◆ *chūban* ◆ Tokyo National Museum

Osen, daughter of the proprietor of a teahouse in the grounds of the Kasamori Shrine, was the "Miss Edo" of her day. Here she is shown seated in front of the shop, in conversation with a good-looking youth selling fans bearing the crest of a leading actor of the day. Harunobu did a number of prints showing Osen. She was a favorite subject of other ukiyo-e artists also; she appeared in prints and picture books, and even on broadsheets and hand towels.

74

45. "The Motoyanagi Store" ◆ *chūban* ◆ Private collection

This print and that shown in Plate 46 both depict Ofuji, daughter of the proprietor of Motoyanagi's, one of the toothpick shops that stood behind the temple of Kannon in Asakusa. Her beauty, second only to that of Osen (Plate 44), is said to have made Harunobu throw down his brush in despair on several occasions—though to the modern eye at least her face differs little from those of the other beauties shown in Harunobu's prints. She was also known as the "gingko girl," because of the gingko trees that stood near the shop.

46. "Morning Haze at Asakusa" from "Eight Sophisticated Views of Edo" ◆ *chūban* ◆ Private collection

In this print, Ofuji is seen in conversation with a handsome young samurai. The toothpick shop is much the same as it is shown in the preceding print, and to make doubly sure that Ofuji, the "gingko girl," should be recognized, Harunobu has strewn a few gingko leaves in the foreground.

76

47. "The Reflection" ◈ *chūban* ◈ Tokyo National Museum

A *komusō*—one of the wandering monks who, with baskets over their heads, strolled about the country playing the flute—has stopped to play before what appears to be a house in the gay quarters. A courtesan has come out to hear him and—in a typical ukiyo-e conceit that gives the picture its point—has caught sight of his face, reflected in the water that stands on the veranda. He is, of course, young and good-looking.

48. "Musumefū" from "A Posy of Beauties from the Floating World" ◆ *chūban* ◆ Tokyo National Museum

A typical Harunobu scene showing a young man and young woman with faces that are beautiful yet scarcely distinguishable from each other. The bush clover from which the young man is breaking a sprig is one of the conventional indications of autumn.

49. "Sumō in the Corridor" ◆ *chūban* ◆ Seiichirō
Takahashi Collection

This print, one of many scenes by Harunobu
showing children at play, is typical in its charm and
gentle humor. The young woman with the fan is,
of course, taking the part of the *gyōji*, the "referee"
who supervises each bout of sumō wrestling.

50. "The Spreading Plum-Tree" ◆ *chūban* ◆ Tokyo National Museum

The scene is a plum garden. A young woman holding a *kiseru*—the long-stemmed, small-bowled pipe popular in Japan until well into the present century—is getting a light from a handsome young dandy. In its romanticism and its combination of mild eroticism and a feeling of extreme innocence the print is utterly typical of Harunobu's work as a whole.

80

51. "Shuttlecock and Battledore" ❖ *chūban* ❖
Takaharu Mitsui Collection

In a scene very similar—even to the plum blossom in the background—to that of the preceding

plate, a young man and woman are shown playing
shuttlecock and battledore. Never the most vigorous of sports, the game here is clearly only a pretext
for a little romantic dalliance.

52. "A Tale Told on the Veranda" ◆ *chūban* ◆ Tokyo National Museum

Two young lovers, thinking they are alone, are whispering sweet nothings to each other on the veranda facing the garden, while another young woman, unbeknown to them, is eavesdropping through the partly opened sliding doors leading to the room beyond. Again, the faces of the lovers have the same remote, childlike and—in one sense—utterly sexless faces as those in Harunobu's other prints. The introduction of an eavesdropper is typical of the small, often slightly titillating twists that uki-yo-e artists often used to give variety to what was a comparatively restricted range of subjects.

53. "High Geta in the Snow" ◆ *chūban* ◆ Tokyo National Museum

It is snowing, and the young woman, who is wearing rounded, black-lacquered *geta* of the kind known as *pokkuri*, is having difficulty in walking along the riverside path. Her younger companion is removing the snow from the *geta* for her, using the end of her fan.

56. "The Second Month" from "Seasonal Poems in Contemporary Settings" ◆ *chūban* ◆ Tokyo National Museum

Here, one of the pictures of children of which Harunobu was so fond is used to symbolize the second month. The drum and a shrine banner that the four boys are carrying indicate that the date is the first "Horse Day" of the second month according to the Oriental zodiacal calendar, the day on which Inari shrines (Shintō shrines dedicated to the fox god) throughout the country held a regular festival.

86

57. "The Third Month" from "Seasonal Poems in Contemporary Settings" ◆ *chūban* ◆ Seiichirō Taka-hashi Collection

A young man and woman are gathering shells at low tide. The poem reads: "Shells of every possible hue are gathered on the shore, turning it into a veritable beach of brocade."

60. "The Sixth Month" from "Seasonal Poems in Contemporary Settings" ◆ *chūban* ◆ Seiichirō Takahashi Collection

The rainy season is over, summer is at its height, and a young samurai is taking his ease in the eve- ning at a teahouse overlooking the river, while gay pleasure boats go past outside. "Here by the river, the waves lap at the bank and the breeze is cool: How should one feel like going home?"

風俗四季哥仙

立秋

みかけぬ

笑りを

れも

天の川

あせ川

ま乃

一夜

きれ

とも

鈴木春信画

61. "The Beginning of Autumn" from "Seasonal Poems in Contemporary Settings" ◆ *chūban* ◆ Sei-ichirō Takahashi Collection

In front of the houses visible beyond the window one can see fronds of bamboo with gaily-colored paper decorations tied to them—a sign that it is the seventh of the seventh month, the day of the Tanabata Festival. According to Chinese and Japanese legend, it is on this day—as the poem reminds us—that the Herdsboy and the Weaver, heavenly lovers who are separated all the rest of the year by the Milky Way, are reunited for one brief night of love.

62. "The Eighth Month" from "Seasonal Poems in Contemporary Settings" ◆ *chūban* ◆ Seiichirō Takahashi Collection

This extremely beautiful print captures perfectly the conventional, romantic view of autumn in Harunobu's day. The *hagi* blossom is in full bloom, the harvest moon is at its most beautiful in the sky above, and a stream in which to view the moon's reflection flows conveniently close at hand. The two young women, one of whom wears a kimono with an appropriate design of maple leaves, are combining the pleasures of moon-viewing and incense-smelling.

63. "The Ninth Month" from "Seasonal Poems in Contemporary Settings" ◆ *chūban* ◆ Tokyo National Museum

The young man who, appropriately enough, holds a vase of freshly picked chrysanthemums (the old name for the ninth month of the lunar calendar was "chrysanthemum month") seems to be wooing his reluctant companion, while within the house one of the eavesdroppers whom Harunobu seems to have liked to portray peers out curiously from the partly opened sliding screens.

風俗四季哥仙
神無月

僑りのつれなき世なりけり神無月さりゆく澤うるさら初むらん

64. "The Tenth Month" from "Seasonal Poems in Contemporary Settings" ◆ *chūban* ◆ Seiichirō Takahashi Collection

Autumn is drawing to a close, as is shown by the bright maple leaves that stand in the vase on the veranda. It is already chilly enough for the young man to have a charcoal brazier by his side, and the rain falling outside doubtless heightens the melancholy he feels as he reads the long love letter he holds in his hands.

65. "The Eleventh Month" from "Seasonal Poems in Contemporary Settings" ◆ *chūban* ◆ Seiichirō Takahashi Collection

The scene, which shows a whole family—mother, father, and child—on their way to see a local Shintō shrine festival, is rather unusual for an ukiyo-e print. The gay vermilion of the *torii* gateway, and the relaxed, festive atmosphere make this one of the happiest of all Harunobu's prints.

95

66. "The Twelfth Month" from "Seasonal Poems in Contemporary Settings" ♦ *chūban* ♦ Seiichirō Takahashi Collection

The poem appended to this charming picture of children playing in the snow runs: "I will take care to leave the snow in the garden as it is, without so much as a footprint. May it not melt until some visitor comes to see it!"